Match Them
Nursery Rhymes

Ding Dong Bell

By Ronald Ridout

Illustrated by Karen Tushingham

Collins
in association with
Belitha Press

Dear Adult,

Here is a series of colourful and entertaining write-in books aimed at introducing nursery and infant children of 3-6 to basic recognition of words and phrases.

The **Match Them ... Words** books (ages 3-5) will help children to learn about their immediate environment while the **Match Them ... Nursery Rhymes** books (ages 4-6) will enable children to discover new words within a familiar context. They will also help children who are learning the rhymes for the first time!

At first, you will need to show the child how to link the word to the picture or space, but they will soon get the idea of matching for themselves, and will enjoy doing the exercises unaided.

Within each book there is a gradual progression, so that as children gain confidence, they can tackle something a little harder. Some words and matching pictures appear in both the **Words** and **Nursery Rhymes** books – and every child will have fun spotting them and so reinforce their learning!

Ronald Ridout

First published 1988 by William Collins Sons & Co Ltd
in association with Belitha Press Limited,
31 Newington Green, London N16 9PU
Text and illustrations in this format copyright © Belitha Press 1988
Text copyright © Ronald Ridout 1988
Illustrations copyright © Karen Tushingham 1988
Art Director: Treld Bicknell   Editor: Carol Watson
All rights reserved. No part of this publication may be reproduced in any form whatsoever without the permission of the publishers and the copyright holders.
ISBN 0 00 197728 8
10 9 8 7 6 5 4 3 2 1
Typesetting by Chambers Wallace, London
Printed by Purnell Book Production Limited, Paulton, England, for Imago

Little Jack Horner

Little Jack Horner
Sat in a corner,
Eating a Christmas pie;
He put in his thumb,
And pulled out a plum,
And said, 'What a good boy am I!'

Can you match the words and pictures?
Begin like this:

Little Jack Horner
Sat in a corner,
Eating a Christmas pie;

He put in his thumb,

And pulled out a plum,
And said,
'What a good boy am I!'

3

Ding dong bell

Ding, dong, bell,
Pussy's in the well.
Who put her in?
Little Johnny Green.
Who pulled her out?
Little Tommy Stout.
What a naughty boy was that
To try to drown poor pussy cat,
Who never did him any harm,
But killed the mice in his father's barn.

Can you match the picture to the space?
Begin like this:

Ding, dong ____,

Pussy's in the ____.

Who put her in?

_____ _____ _____.

Who pulled her out?

_____ _____ _____.

What a naughty boy was that

To try to drown poor ____,

Who never did him any harm,

But killed the mice in his father's barn.

Whose footsteps are these?

One, two, buckle my shoe

One, two,
Buckle my shoe;

Three, four,
Knock at the door;

Five, six,
Pick up sticks;

Seven, eight,
Lay them straight;

Nine, ten,
A big fat hen.

Can you match the words to the pictures?   Begin like this:

One, two,
Buckle my   ;   sticks

Three, four,
Knock at the   ;

                                                                  shoe

Five, six,
Pick up   ;

Seven, eight,   hen
Lay them straight;

Nine, ten,
A big fat   .
                                                                  door

How many hens can you count?

7

Little Boy Blue

Little Boy Blue,
Come blow your horn,
The sheep's in the meadow,
The cow's in the corn.

Where is the boy
Who looks after the sheep?
He's under a haystack
Fast asleep.

Will you wake him?
No, not I,
For if I do
He's sure to cry.

Can you match the words to the pictures?   Begin like this:

Little Boy Blue,

Come blow your ,

The 's in the meadow,

The 's in the corn.

But where is the

Who looks after the ?

He's under a
Fast asleep.

Will you wake him?
No, not I,
For if I do
He's sure to cry.

Old Mother Hubbard

Old Mother Hubbard
Went to the cupboard
To fetch her poor dog a bone.
When she got there
The cupboard was bare,
And so the poor dog had none.

She went to the hatter's
To buy him a hat.
When she came back,
He was feeding the cat.

She went to the tailor's
To buy him a coat.
When she came back,
He was riding a goat.

Can you match the words to the pictures? Begin like this:

Old Mother Hubbard

Went to the    dog

To fetch her poor dog a .

When she got there   cupboard

The cupboard was bare,

And so the poor  had none.   hat

She went to the hatter's

To buy him a .   bone

When she came back,

He was feeding the  .

She went to the tailor's   goat

To buy him a coat.

When she came back,

He was riding a .   cat

11

Sing a song of sixpence

Sing a song of sixpence,
A pocket full of rye;
Four and twenty blackbirds,
Baked in a pie.

When the pie was opened,
The birds began to sing,
Wasn't that a dainty dish,
To set before the king?

The king was in his counting-house,
Counting out his money,
The queen was in the parlour,
Eating bread and honey.

The maid was in the garden,
Hanging out the clothes,
When down came a blackbird
And pecked off her nose.

Find the missing words.   Begin like this:

Sing a song of sixpence,

A pocket full of rye;

Four and twenty [blackbirds],   money

Baked in a [pie].

When the pie was opened,   king

The birds began to sing,

Wasn't that a dainty dish,

To set before the [king]?

The king was in the counting-house,

Counting out his [money],   pie

The [queen] was in the parlour,

Eating bread and honey.   queen

The maid was in the [garden],

Hanging out the clothes,   garden

When down came a blackbird

And pecked off her nose.

13

Rock-a-bye baby

Rock-a-bye baby, on the tree top,
When the wind blows, the cradle will rock;
When the bough breaks, the cradle will fall,
And down will come baby and cradle and all.

Can you find the missing word? Begin like this:

Rock-a-bye ____,

on the ____ top,

When the wind blows,

the ____ will rock;

When the ____ breaks,

the cradle will fall,

And down will come ____,

cradle and all.

tree

baby

bough

baby

cradle

Wee Willie Winkie

Wee Willie Winkie runs through the town,
Upstairs and downstairs in his night-gown,
Rapping at the window, crying through the lock,
Are all the children in their beds,
For now it's eight o'clock?

Can you join up the dots to see Willie Winkie?

Ladybird, ladybird, fly away home

Ladybird, ladybird,
Fly away home,
Your house is on fire
And your children are gone;
All except one
And that's little Ann
And she has crept under
The frying pan.

Have your child cut out and color the shape below.
Help your child to write his or her phone number on it.

7

Can you find the missing words? Begin like this:

Ladybird, ____,

Fly away home,

Your ____ is on ____

And your children are gone;

All except ____

And that's little Ann

And she has crept under

The frying ____.

house

pan

fire

one

ladybird

Can you help the ladybird find little Ann?

I had a little nut tree

I had a little nut tree,
Nothing would it bear
But a silver nutmeg
And a golden pear;
The king of Spain's daughter
Came to visit me,
And all for the sake
Of my little nut tree.
I skipped over water,
I danced over sea,
And all the birds in the air
Couldn't catch me.

Can you find the missing words?   Begin like this:

I had a little ____ ____,

Nothing would it bear

But a silver ____

And a golden ____;

The king of Spain's daughter

Came to visit me,

And all for the sake

Of my little nut tree.

I skipped over water,

I danced over ____,

And all the ____ in the air

Couldn't catch me.

nutmeg

birds

pear

nut tree

sea

19

A farmer went trotting

A farmer went trotting upon his grey mare,
Bumpety, bumpety, bump!
With his daughter behind him so rosy and fair,
Lumpety, lumpety, lump.
A raven cried, Croak! and they all tumbled down,
Bumpety, bumpety, bump!
The mare broke her knees and the farmer his crown,
Lumpety, lumpety, lump!

Can you find the missing words?   Begin like this:

A farmer went trotting upon his grey ____,   raven

Bumpety, bumpety, bump!

With his daughter behind him so rosy and fair,   down

Lumpety, lumpety, lump!

A ____ cried, Croak! and they all tumbled ____,   mare

Bumpety, bumpety, bump!

The ____ broke her knees and the ____ his crown,   farmer

Lumpety, lumpety, lump!

mare

Can you colour us?

I had a little pony

I had a little pony,
His name was Dapple Gray;
I lent him to a lady
To ride a mile away.

She whipped him, she slashed him.
She rode him through the mire;
I would not lend my pony now,
For all the lady's hire.

Can you find the missing words?   Begin like this:

I had a little ___,

His ___ was Dapple Gray;

I lent him to a ___

To ride a mile away.

She whipped ___, she slashed him,

She ___ him through the mire;

I would not lend my ___ now

For all the lady's hire.

him

pony

name

rode

pony

lady

Rhyme puzzle

This rhyme is muddled up.
Can you match the sentences
to the right picture?

She went to the hatter's
To buy him a hat.
When she came back,
He was feeding the cat.

She went to the tailor's
To buy him a coat.
When she came back,
He was riding a goat.

Old Mother Hubbard
Went to the cupboard
To fetch her poor dog a bone.
When she got there,
The cupboard was bare,
And so the poor dog had none.